QUEEN PALM

Nancy Anne Miller is a Bermudian poet with ten
published collections, including *Pink Typewriter*
(Kelsay Books, April 2023). Her poetry has been
published internationally in journals such as
Edinburgh Review, *Poetry Ireland Review*, *The Moth*,
Salzburg Review, *Agenda*, *Stand*, *Magma*, *Ambit*,
The Fiddlehead, *Dalhousie Review*, *The International
Literary Quarterly* and *The Caribbean Writer*, among
many others. She has an MLitt in Creative Writing
from the University of Glasgow. She organized the
Ber-Mused poetry reading for Bermuda's 400th
anniversary in 2009, is a MacDowell Fellow, and
Bermuda Arts Council Grant recipient.

Queen Palm

A Bermuda Christmas

POEMS *by*

Nancy Anne Miller

VP

Valley Press

First published in 2023 by Valley Press
Woodend, The Crescent, Scarborough, UK, YO11 2PW
www.valleypressuk.com

ISBN 978-1-915606-37-2
Cat. no. VP0223

A CIP record for this book is available from the British Library.

Cover photograph by Jennifer Boyer.
Cover and text design by Jamie McGarry.

Printed and bound in Great Britain by
Imprint Digital, Upton Pyne, Exeter.

Contents

for Art

Because the mountain grass
Cannot but keep the form
Where the mountain hare has lain

'Memory', W.B. Yeats

'All the Christmases roll down toward the two-tongued sea'
A Child's Christmas in Wales, Dylan Thomas

'The Iliad of peace began
when this girl agreed'
'Animal Nativity', Les Murray

THE OIL OF MIRTH

Queen Palm

The Christmas lights twirl
around the palm, the path
of a hula hoop or of ice swirled
in a glass. I think of a slinky,

slinking. The long torso, scaled
as a mermaid's fishy body,
the lower trunk curved as if
to rest from a long swim.

Transparent white bulbs,
X-ray of the pliant vertebrae
needed by island women to
bend, sway, and to stand tall.

Allowed

The woman selling the wreaths asks me if I want a bow.
I said, *No, I am from an island!* To myself I say, *My mother*

taught me to hate red. Although when I look at a floppy
plastic one, I am reminded of squirrel fish adorning reefs

off South Shore with their bright fins and gills. Missing
one primary colour, I went for pink. The sands of Bermuda

are soft as flesh, and I lay on them like on a mother's belly
with the rim of a wave touching my toes, surf dropping water

on the beach, a woman before labour. I have learned
to let the wreath do its dance round and round, a mothering

circle, or an antiphon. An 'O' on the side of my house sings
to the heavens: yellow stars, blue night, two colours allowed.

Packwood Rest Home

Here we are at Packwood,
straw hats sift sunlight
onto our faces, bright as tears.

Here we are at Packwood,
runners on the rockers
tip into our conversation,

like commas slowing it down.
Here we are at Packwood,
look out to sea, where

the tide is thrown down,
like a woman doing laundry.
She rolls and unrolls,

pounds to make clean.
Here we are at Packwood,
eat Cassava Pie at Christmas,

made from bitter African roots,
we sweeten for the holidays,
push through cookery netting,

strain and strain again,
until it blends well with
eggs, white sugar, and allspice.

Cassava Roots at the West Indian Fair

The child from St. Kitts runs around,
carries a lone cassava root on her

shoulder like a teddy bear, while
the market woman holds a cluster of

them, sprawling teats over the scale's pram.
Gangly as a banana bunch from Bermuda,

multi-limbed octopus, many appendages,
needs to be approached with caution.

The cluster I hold is multi-armed,
a Buddhist goddess, requires a process,

rituals of many washings, beatings.
Contains a blessing, contains a curse.

Heaped on the table is a mound of animal
faeces. Singular, a mole absorbs the dark

of African soil. A spearhead from a tribe
hammered into a clumsy blade missing

a stick. Needs intensive labour, care to be
brought to the table, to be properly served.

Flight from Egypt

Something must be slain,
the brown poisonous skin peeled, so
white meat emerges as a purity, as

layers bow over to the process, when
a blade frees. Nature guards its
treasures. A multi-fingered vegetable,

like an African diaspora of countries
dependent on a hardy crop in
unnourished soils. Mimics the flight

from Egypt, modest beginnings
made princely. A gold batter of
eggs, sugar, butter adorns Christmas

Cassava Pie. Clumsy, square,
crusted, a large British saddle bag
opens, full of a Caribbean journey.

Christmas Trees at Home and Abroad

The first Christmas tree I see
this year is in front of St. John's,
in Washington, CT, with one string
of lights. It has the clumsy
innocence of a child's drawing.

The second one is at the liquor
store in Bantam, CT, over-decorated,
plump, cut off by the top and
bottom of the window.
A beer belly hangs out.

The third is on the porch of
the country store, Dorset, VT,
cards tied to each branch, like
young girls would wrap hair
in paper to curl at night.

The last one is a stately palm
in Paget, BDA, waist held in
tightly by a corset of sparkle,
large fronds wave arms,
welcome all wayfarers home.

Sea-Through

The Garden Centre employee,
Nick, throws the tree onto my Jag,
and ties it through opened
windows, tightens twine like the girth

of a saddle. This tree will transport
me into the holiday season. It is a rocket
ready to launch from my moving vehicle.
It miraculously stands up straight and tall

at seven feet, like a metronome centring. I
adorn it with island pink, turquoise balls,
much seen in seafood huts on the coast, often
enmeshed in fish nets, where wind chimes

made from thin shells hang from doors,
like a sole earring on a privateer. How we
bring our home with us wherever we are,
like Christ brought heaven to earth. I used

to swim underwater in the harbour, hear
boats bobbing, buoys teeming, sounds
like gears changing in a large rusty machine,
the sea, the mechanics, the force in my universe.

The Oil of Mirth

As I drive through a Christmas landscape,
the bright metallic sound of a Steel Band
chimes carols, resonates in my car as if
it were a drum. The oil of mirth is
my fuel, much like gas the Shell barrels
held. I travel warmly over hill, dale.

Windshield wipers conduct, guide
the music. Fan-shaped as a percussion
brush; they go back, forward, rock
in the rhythm of an island metronome.
The flurry of a page turner, swooshes snow
away as I do when I move to the seasoned sounds.

Bermuda Christmas

Stars above Bermuda strewn a watery dark,
bivalve molluscs rinsed bright from a salty tide.

Pink, orange, yellow houses lined with lights,
ribbons around Christmas parcels. The chimney

awaits Santa's slippage down, fat belly, round
as a cherry bomb. Explodes the parlour into

ripped boxes, torn paper. Town's traffic signals,
advent globes, blink the season's red, green over

taxi journeys. The way a sprig of holly makes
the day merry. Once again, the island intersects

heaven, earth. Morris Minors pass, topped with trees,
the spikey fins of a green parrotfish cut sky's shoals. Will

stand inside, multi-arms bob white bulbs, glow like octopus
suckers emit bioluminescence in the deep ocean.

Corsage

The palm trees lit with Christmas bulbs:
pink, turquoise, orange explode like
fireworks against the humid island sky,
a carnival street welcome on my return

to the isle as the taxi takes me away from
the airport. They line the route out of
the parking lot, horrific as underwater
sponges with spiney torsos, Kitchen Maid

rubber glove fingers sift the sky like water.
More celebratory than a solemn Advent
tree such as the green Balsam Fir, full
of scent as it dies in bright funeral clothes,

presents beneath, a distraction. Arced
in giving, the palm drops gifts of fruit
through the year. Now is a gigantic corsage
pinned to the isle, for motherhood, for fussing.

Island Christmas

The music of the Christmas carols
played on island steel drums
is tinny, bright, sharp
as my metallic Mexican ornaments.

They flash colour off angles,
prickly as fins of tropical fish.
Cow Polly, Parrot, and Angelfish
swim waves of green bobbing branches.

At the bottom of the trunk
is a stack of wrapped presents,
hidden as the sunken treasure
from a lost Bermudian vessel.

The one I open is wrapped in
layers of plastic bubble, an ice pack
to preserve the orange loquat jam
from May's kitchen and orchard.

Island gifts always contain an absence,
like the dead starfish I find on
a South Shore Beach, lying limp
as a bow off a package.

Omission

My brothers picked off each Christmas bulb
along the cedar ceiling beam with a new BB gun.
The jaws of the ornaments hung open as our mouths
when we thought of mother's care decorating.
She thoughtfully measured distances, tried to make it
even as the love she distributed to four children.
She and Edwards, the gardener, used the same precision
to plant flowers along the stone wall of an island garden.
The broken edges of the globes now shone in the dark
like stars that quickly routed the day off course.

The glass, shiny as sequins, was dispersed over the floor,
coiled around the presents like a snake's shed skin.
Tiny splinters cut our hands when we cleaned up,
made bloody fingerprints. So afraid, I kept
my new doll in her box; she gazed kindly through
the plastic front like a saint in a grotto. I threw
the gun overboard, watched it sink into turquoise,
go down under the folds of the watery tissue-paper.
And kept my silence to keep the family peace; like
Mary, I trusted the angels to fill in with the details.

Full

I bring the empty Tropicana
Bottle, now full of water, to the tree
like an IV to keep it refreshed.

I pour the rest of it out.
Enough to keep a villager
alive in Kenya, the braided

stream an umbilical cord.
We collected the rain on
our roofs in Bermuda, kept

it in a tank with a palmetto leaf,
shaped like an open peacock's
tail, proud to be so full.

Boxing Day

Out of the box finally,
Christmas day over,
fall out bits of sparkle
present from the gathering.

Advent, a house party of sorts
in ancient days when adoring
Magi, Shepherds showed
when they could. An extra day

necessary after aiming for
the one moment, like the star
over Bethlehem is a target;
when truly its light is

the jagged ripped paper
from a gift package. We
need another 24 hours to put
the long year to sleep with

this bedtime story for both
child, adult. Hear again
about the birth of a baby,
who opened up the world.

Gombey

The drumsticks beat so fast,
so fast, are the hands
of a clock come undone,
because this is no time,
no time, a day of freedom,
to dance the streets of Bermuda.

The tall feathers of the hat,
crisscross like the top of
a tent, as underneath a body
moves through parishes in
this shelter pitched for the day,
dwells in African music.

Tiny mirrors reflect light,
water shaken from one
baptized in the sea. Shillings
thrown down by a master
to purchase a slave, to own,
but not on Boxing Day.

Springs out of a corner,
bright Christmas wrapping,
goes missing in living colour,
acts out Biblical stories. David,
Goliath, Daniel in the lion's den.

VISITATION

Arrival

And so it does, modestly on the stamps
I buy with the holy family in flight,
frames of a film strip of that trip
still leaving tracks across our lives.

Unassuming, a human burden borne
on a donkey. The beast that will
bear boxes, cards, documents for the
Royal Post through the years ahead.

A living letter, this child enveloped in
swaddling clothes. The Word made
flesh escapes editing. Herod's desire
to cross out any history, but his own.

First Christmas Card

So fitting my first Christmas card
comes from a trash man; drags
the large plastic bag towards
the dumpster, engine revs,
steams, a snorting beast.

Santa away with my rubbish,
what to discard in this season
of giving, do without.
His three magi card,
surely will hit the heap.

Cigarette in hand like a pencil
an elf uses to write down my
Christmas list. The smoke
curls around his chin
into a paste on St. Nick's beard.

The wise men on the greeting
look up at the star,
seek a treasure in heaven.
I empty garbage weekly into a plastic
lined can, dark as any black hole.

Visitation

The iron rod hits the mailbox
so hard, the young man
must be trying to hammer
the post into the ground.

The red flag falls,
a dumbfounded animal's
tongue sticks out in awe.
Mail scatters, the world

shaken like a snow globe.
Lumpy as Santa's sack,
my box spills catalogues:
J. Crew, L.L. Bean, Garnet Hill,

Sundance, Company Store, J. Jill,
Saks, The Vermont Country Store
announce again the holiday season.
I pick up these spread cards,

my playing partner gone,
think of him wielding his weapon.
A letter opener unseals
my steel-white roadside envelope

crammed far too full. Think
of the hand he dealt me,
and bless his avenging sword,
bless him, my holy night visitor.

Landing Strip

The roof is a landing strip for Santa,
or angels on the way with Good News.

Lights even out the roof's line, make it
safe and approachable by a wide sleigh.

The chimney is the airplane trafficker's
tower, smoke spreads its labyrinth map.

The flames' ragged heart waves the flight in.
Santa leaves his packages below, then is

up the narrow neck, where warmth
rises like mercury in a thermometer.

He emerges in his red fireman's suit,
after he set the whole household alight.

Tag

The farmer no longer allows
people to tie a string or bow
on the Christmas tree, come
back later to cut it down.

Others remove the ribbon,
claim it for themselves,
in a game of 'It' where
being caught is to end

with the runt fir. We take
labels off articles we give
others as presents, try to
capture the who we think

they are. Shopkeepers replace
them when a gift is returned.
In this game of tag, we try to
touch, be touched by others.

Payback

She is having a smoke while she rings the bell,
squats down by the pot, a kettle warming up
over a fire under the bridges where she slept.

I slip a five-dollar bill in a Philips screwdriver
slot, a mini cross to unlock the woes of poverty,
help a homeless person in the mall's December chill.

A red bag hangs between the vein of ropes,
plasma to infuse the nearly-dead, buckets of
blood shed to revitalize numbness. Notes chime

like dropped coins, scatter a parking lot, against
K Mart windows, over McDonald's camel
humps, slip into the heart, open up a purse.

Wreath on House

It keeps sliding down from weight,
the largest one to buy, hangs on
a ribbon, a self-congratulatory medal.

Goes missing, rolling down the hill,
an extra tire on a motor home,
flips, lands, grounded bird's nest.

Once again, I lift the green circle to
the front window, bound by a wire noose,
try to fit this round peg in a square hole.

Christmas Landscape

Red Christmas bows turn lamppost,
house, dog into festive presents.
Waves of green on fences fall,
rise in peaks to wreaths like life
preservers. Bob in an ocean, as we
ride the tides of the season, try to

stay afloat. We collect branches
in urns, fresh, fragrant, verdant,
as the landscape becomes marbled
with the lined ruins of dead foliage.
Cards arrive in the mail, the flap,
the peaked roof of a church,

bring messaged praise. Even
the robust snowman has been
given a scarf, jacket, boots,
gloves to wear before he,
like the homeless, disappears
into winter's clean-up act.

Relief

Like the trees would rather have not
gotten out of bed this morning. They
are half-dressed, stand as if in a doorway
with piles of dead leaves at their feet,
days of uncollected mail on the porch.

They had quite a party through late
October, dressed for fun, to shine in
the dark when a car's headlights made them stars.
They burnt themselves out performing in front
of so many fans, strangers. They deserve

the moment to not be noticed. No one gazes
at them now, but look straight ahead as they
drive by. They must be relieved to think
Christmas trees will now have the attention,
the burden of cheering the masses placed elsewhere.

Before

It is all about cleaning up,
large shovels on the town
truck slam the bank.

Scoop! Swirling lights
send dancing angels
around my dining room

as 12x12 panes twirl,
as if to come inside
and to clean up too.

I need them as I turn
the fireplace into
a stable in my mind.

Grate with wood, the manger,
fire the light of the child.
A real clean-it-all-up act!

If this isn't working for you,
then let's just leave it
with the windows reflecting

on the walls like molars,
and I'm in the jaws of winter.
Shovels outside

on the truck eat up snow,
like some dinosaur did before
Christmas was ever born.

Unplug the Tree

Let it twirl out from the string of lights,
a top spins to the edge of the room.

Unplug from the socket, dented pig's snout.
Pick up broken glass ornaments, apples

bitten into, discarded, at a feast with
too many choices. Known as she-balsam,

milked for resin, nursed presents, bows
soft as ears under a branch. Now tilts,

tipsy as a late-night party hat. Has another
life waiting outside, will drop needles one by

one into a golden haystack, like a mock-up
frock comes undone as pins unloosen.

Letting Go of Christmas

The Christmas Trees on my bank
account statement, imprinted red

and green reach a climatic point.
Two breasts nurture the flow of

the season. Santa's Elves take off felt
work caps. Numbers reveal what is left,

the ones recorded below what now
looks like two mountains of rising debt.

The Afterlife of Christmas Trees

No longer like rockets about to ascend,
supercharging homes with brightness, merriment,
they stand at windows, unlit, like carousels turned

off. Lights no longer guiding one round and
round into a spin, the twirl of season spirits
up, down. Now a present emerges which won't

fit under a tree, but needs all the boxes of
a calendar, where the owner stuffs them full,
then ticks off each with a tidy bow. Now

trees stand quietly, still dressed, look out,
water flower-ish, avoiding a dance, seek
the time before they were swept off their feet.

A POET'S CHRISTMAS

Wreath

Surprised by how large it is,
it comes in three sections,
each one curved into the puffy
breast of a shot pheasant.

The joiner's steel mouths,
curved like the goatskin flasks
shepherds drank from. Such bounty.
I put it in front of my hearth,

the spiral of Celtic green.
a mothering circle. Round as
a belly button, a mouth, a nipple.
I could not adorn a tree this year

where a Christmas bulb might fall,
break. The Times Square Ball.
Remind me as they bounced
in the waves of the tree, how

fragile each year is. I prefer
this rotund roundness, camels,
and angels alike ride a carousel
which merrily blurs all endings.

Glass Ceiling

Without Christmas wreaths, trees
to cheer it up, the New Year
folds around Holiday Greetings
like a large white envelope.

Snow falls in brittle pieces,
a glass ceiling shatters as if
an angel hit it, flying back to
Heaven after Annunciation duties.

I lie on the ground, wave
my arms back and forth, leave
the shape of wings, a fossil
imprint of when I once could fly.

I am glad that I can't, don't. I
make holes in the white, body
weight crunches down as even
my breath turns to ice, has volume.

A Poet's Christmas

Drive rutted road, tires deep
in snow, car a metal zipper.
Unzips loose fabric of

a melting season. Patches of
white left, right, discarded
sheets of paper from a present.

What in me wants to close,
instead of open? Be the sealed
envelope, not the bright card,

announcing Advent? Where
the Wise Woman? Looks up,
prepares with gifts ahead,

sure of the sky's signals,
knows when to stop, start,
at one with celestial traffic?

I'm the shepherdess instead,
eyes routed to the ground,
heavens have to warn via

a terrible messenger, who
blocks my path, sirens
blare, stars pop like emergency

fire flares to arrest, tell me
something has happened
abroad, something worth notice.

Colour Blind

A silver is omnipresent, but not
just for the lining; rather the tone
of the sky is an unpolished grey.

I am unfamiliar with a barren hue,
coming from an island where
turquoise seas outwitted the blue

above, where there was no
closing act for brilliance. Here
applause is given for the odd

shiny bits in the woods. As if
the trees have thrown down
coins to pay for summer's fullness.

I try to join a Thanksgiving heart,
be grateful for the vision a dullness
imparts. So, when yellow, pink,

orange Christmas lights shine
everywhere, I am so grateful,
as if a blindfold has been removed.

Unwrapped

Like unwrapped presents,
everything is exposed,
not covered; no snow abounds
to drape the world in mystery.

Christmas tree lights
on Main Street look
like forced fruit perfectly
produced in hothouses.

Global warming and
the greenhouse effect
remove even the boxed
container of a season.

When spring no longer
arrives, because the robin
carries a piece of straw
in its beak like a ribbon.

A sign to us of the earth's
opening. What will be left
for us to wait for, and to
surprise us with its contents?

Red

Wreath on New England door
with Christmas ribbon, red bird
on a springtime nest. Two

of them flew about the sky
this morning in a mating game,
darted with the quickness and deft of

a mime artist's hands. Here a tail
feather dropped, rose petal,
blood blushes winter's ice cheek.

Christmas Week, Washington CT

The bare apple trees in Averill's
Orchard contort like Pilobolus
Dancers in one of their performances.

The Congregational Church with
its spire is an origami sculpture,
folded white, neatens into a holiness

of angles. I see a man kneeling
before a maple tapping it in
December, like a pilgrim waiting

for a stigmata. The season's warmth
unpredictable, everything reveals
a new form as the earth unwraps layers.

Ever Green

Like a too-early guest,
the tree arrives weeks
before expected. I make
it comfortable, give it a drink.

Unnoticed by me, strung
quickly with lights, like
a flapper would wind around,
neck, body in the twenties, eager

to be gay, full of youth, ever green,
and with too much perfume.
It will be noticed by a fragrance
I don't see. A priestess fills the house

with incense, arms lifted to praise.
Meant to stay verdant forever,
it has an autumn, drops needles,
like hair pins, because we desired it.

Unpacking the Tree

This year it is Caesarean style,
I cut the box open regardless
of the silver steel stitching on
the side from a previous

operation. The brown cardboard
hacked and piled up in mounds,
as if I dug through dirt to
uproot it. Branches crosshatched

like laces on an old shoe. I cut
the green strings and it moves
into a new step, a ballerina
changes from first to second

position. It is fragrance which
will adorn our lives. Frankincense
and myrrh announced portly
midnight guests. It sits rotund, wise.

Rorschach Test

All kinds of greenery tied with red ribbons,
branches bowed like a horse's tail adorned,
the rosettes of wreaths hang everywhere,
harness the wood's offerings into seasonal ritual.

How patchy the landscape gets after
Christmas, like appaloosas and pied ponies,
mangy distortion of brown puddles on white,
the friskiness of nature unbound.

Intermittently, a snowstorm covers raw
bones with the vanity of hiding gawky
elbows, knees. Furniture draped in
a grand summer room off season.

Except dark lines of trees, estuaries
and tributaries of bark against sky's
blue, map our journey into solace.
The Rorschach tests we dress with meanings.

Christmas Tree

Since we have cut you off from earth,
we will console you with the sky.
Place the farthest star at your top,
have you point to it to guide days.
Wreath you with dawn's rainbow,
place suns and moons across boughs.

Your glow, a mapped constellation
leads a few to birth. When you die
thirsty, lick floors in a quiet flame.
We will drag you over cold banks,
to warm the land with a comet's blaze.

AND THE ANIMALS KNEW

Evidence

It takes an angel to convince
a young virgin she will be
impregnated, wings echo
the span of ovaries inside her
abdomen, like the headless Greek

statue of Samothrace. The mind
needs evidence of the heavenly
as feathers flap, spread, a newly-
opened book in earth's history.
Paintings recite the moment with

tickertape announcements, cherubs
roll around skies' ethereal floor
like clumsy toddlers. Takes a child
in a cousin's womb to convince her
body, as he leapt up, wanted to fly.

Too Many Angels

Too many angels get on my nerves
as I decorate the wreath. They get,
got to fly in and out with their twitter-
speech blurbs, the precursor of comics!

Give me the cows, udders pulled
down into earth as calves sucked,
yanked on their teats, children wanting
their toys. Mooing like moans,

horns on heads because they feel devilish.
And the camels too, the moving
mountains they are on a parched
journey where water sloshes inside.

No wonder the airs, the uppity pinched
face; hump a heap of wealth in such
sparseness. Down here below angels,
their profiles rise up to a pitch, make waves.

Immaculate Conception

We all want it to snow.
Want lighted homes
with manger arrangements

of stars, reindeer, shepherds
to appear above the crisp white.
Like Christmas cards which

arrive in the mail slide out
of immaculate envelopes.
We all want it to snow.

Want the feather flakes
to fly above daily tasks
fill tracks as we prepare

the way, unite our physical
being with heaven as
Mary was surrounded

and silently overcome.
We all want it to snow.
Want backyards pure

enough for visiting holy
messengers. See the glare
of wings flare off the iced oak.

Creche

We make the figures
wooden, immoveable,
stiff in their place.

The story inside the box.
Forget how dark it had
to be for a lone star to lead,

how remote one had to live
for angels to appear as guides.
What wants to birth in me?

In some desolate place
within? What newness
do I have no room for?

Carols, Cakes, and a Calm

The lit stars and lit trees
mimic Christmas cookies
when metaphors exchange
places from too much use.

Thank goodness Santa makes
us guess, obese and flying
dangerously low via reindeer
into chimneys, he plummets

like Houdini. The globe is
fragile, an ornament,
glassy, round, may drop,
countries drip snow, leak.

Meanwhile, carols, cakes
and a calm collect all
the signs, signifiers into
a merriment we hum to.

Nativity

I always wanted the Nativity
to be at the beginning of the year,
a small light in a stable, like a flame
in a fireplace warming it up.

I always wanted the baby Jesus to
have twelve months to grow into.
Not have his birth overridden by
some adult new year celebration.

I get that the wise men looked
on the event outside of time, looked
into the heavens for the full arc
of what it would mean through the ages.

And those shepherds, confident,
I'm sure, that following the ways
of sheep would lead them
to the right manger. Their crooks

curled over at the top, like
necks might bend while
they slept on their feet until
the music of angels woke them.

So, we look up or we look down,
to find new life, sneaking in
on a beast known for being
stubborn, and for digging heels in.

The Wise Men

The wise men waited their turn,
used to the sky's slow messages of
night-brailed stars. Shot in slurred
light years, across a silence so vast
one had to be guided. This one

heavy star, swollen with a glow,
hung in its own path, like a bridal
veil pinned, invited the three guests,
steady with gifts. Reluctant to hurry,
until they bore the holy ache of awe.

And the Animals Knew

A place of instinct only,
straw and dung mingle,
cattle are the only
stomping source of heat.

Birds rattle the false
heaven of the eaves.
Lowing rocks the night
slowly as one dark cradle.

A fierce star cuts
a silent path. A child's
cry claims life and
foretells His plea from

death. A young mother
places Him in the first
altar, a crossed wooden
manger. And the animals

knew. Dreamt of days
roaming free out
from the shame of
their blood being let.

Antiphon

I place the wreath into the fire.
It brightens, halo of announcing angel,

floats the flames, leaves a wire circle.
The 'O' in the leaping voice waves

of carols we sing this season.
The 'O' before Star of Wonder,

'O' Come All ye Faithful. 'O'
burnt into lips, Isaiah's coal.

Post-Christmas

I cut the branches from
the un-decorated tree,
shortened limbs make it
a hat rack for passing Advent
visitors. I hold up two pieces
by the bark, spread fans to heed
the fire's flow. They crackle
like a blown electrical fuse,

fill the room with the smell
of incense. Smoke flaps
its amorphous wing, rises
to heaven where stars button
up the dark. I sit in this cave
of light, hear logs move
as they burn, like oxen
shifting haunches in a stable.

And Heaven and Nature Sing

Our voices are flat. The air
let out of all sentences.
The currency of our blood
lit Holiday Greetings up
with an electric glow
during the Christmas Season.

Now, we step into snow as
it descends. The chippings,
shavings from the perfectly
formed Words of The Annunciation,
from which only silence,
so holy and highly could fall.

Annunciation

You know what it is like.
It is a grey day, and the sunset
is a last strip of light,
as the top of a tomb closes.

You know what it is like.
Christmas lights on a bare tree,
a rosary in a hand,
rotating a prayer before nightfall.

You know what it is like.
Wreaths hung on houses
are for the year's funeral,
as it draws to an end.

You know what it is like.
A holiday card you receive
makes you fly up on its wings,
as you spread them wide open.

The Present

Send angels back, hang wings
on bent, iced trees. Remove

wreaths with ornaments, rattle
their glass notes like tambourines.

Undress the Christmas fir, unravel
gay ribbons. Let branches sigh.

Put wrapping away, sweets
we didn't eat. Stripped

of all our garish hopes,
the world opens, white and wide.

Crossed

Like i's dotted, the lit Advent
candles in windows become
birthday lights for the New Year.

A time when individuals do
such, cross t's, look forward
to the Easter one. After winter's

sleet, like bent sails pull towards
a centre, a pilgrim is marked with
a latitude, longitude drawn in ashes.

After

After the angels left
the shepherds
with a sky less bright,
they felt the dark close
around them like folded wings.

I take my tree down,
a heavenly visitor of sorts,
part earth and celestial vision,
feel a space open
that can't be filled with light.

Later in the day,
I find a pointed bow,
the kind we slap on packages,
looped at perfect angles.

I hold it in my hand,
a large fallen star
that still could,
just might lead me somewhere.

Acknowledgements

The following poems have appeared in my former poetry collections:

Latitude, Longitude (Kelsay Books, 2021): 'Flight from Egypt,' 'Christmas Landscape,' 'Post-Christmas,' 'The Afterlife of Christmas Trees,' 'Crossed,' 'Sea-Through'

Tide Tables (Kelsay Books, 2019): 'Corsage,' 'First Christmas Card,' 'Wreath,' 'Relief,' 'Clean Up'

Boiling Hot (Kelsay Books, 2018): 'Un-Plug the Tree,' 'Unpacking the Tree,' 'Christmas Week Washington CT'

Water Logged (Aldrich Press, 2016): 'Cassava Roots at the West Indian Fair,' 'Packwood Rest Home'

Star Map (Futurecycle Press, 2016): 'Rorschach Test'

Immigrant's Autumn (Aldrich Press, 2014): 'Boxing Day,' 'Christmas Trees at Home and Abroad'

Because There Was No Sea (Anapora Literary Press, 2014): 'Oil of Mirth,' 'Maiden Voyage,' 'Bermuda Christmas,' 'Boxing Day'

And in the following journals and anthologies:

The Country and Abroad (USA): 'Boxing Day'

New Ulster (IE): 'Too Many Angels'

Two Countries Anthology (Red Hen Press, USA): 'Christmas Trees at Home and Abroad'

WomanSpeak: A Journal of Art and Literature by Caribbean Women (CAR): 'Queen Palm'

Bermuda Anthology of Poetry II (BDA), *The Caribbean Writer Calendar* (USVI): 'Oil of Mirth'